PUPPY-MILL
SURVIVORS

Melissa McDaniel

the photo book projects: book 4

the
photo book
projects

PRESENT DOG
P R E S S

PUPPY-MILL SURVIVORS | the photo book projects | Melissa McDaniel

Published in 2013 by Present Dog Press

Photographs & text copyright © 2013 Melissa McDaniel
Design & layout copyright © 2013 Present Dog Press
www.thephotobooks.com

the
photo book
projects

ISBN-13: 978-0-9845903-5-3
ISBN-10: 0-9845903-5-8

Designer: Melissa McDaniel

Printer: CPC Solutions
Bookbinder: Roswell Bookbinding

The text of this book was composed in Century Gothic.

Printed and Bound in the USA
10 9 8 7 6 5 4 3 2 1

PRESENT DOG
P   R   E   S   S

Present Dog Press | presentdogpress.com

For my grandmother Elsymae Shepperd & my grandfather Tom Shepperd,

for Sadie,

for Egil Nilsson,

and for all the dogs worldwide
who have suffered, or who are still suffering, in puppy mills

PUTTING AN END TO PUPPY MILLS IS SIMPLE.

DON'T BUY A DOG FROM A PET STORE OR OFF THE INTERNET. THIS STOPS THE DEMAND. IF YOU STOP THE DEMAND, THE MILL OWNERS WILL BE UNABLE TO MAKE MONEY. IF THEY CAN'T MAKE MONEY, THEY WILL CLOSE THE MILLS.

Introduction

TAFFY

In 2009, my boyfriend and I were driving across the U.S. to photograph adopted dogs for my photo book *Rescued in America*. We were just a couple of days into our 5-week road trip when we arrived at a North Carolina home belonging to Cheryl and her mother, Margie. Inside, we were greeted by two adorable Rat Terriers, one male named Aka and a female named Taffy, who was to be photographed by me that day for the book. Little 9-lb. Taffy was a bit nervous that we were there, but she looked excited and happy, too. Most of all, I remember thinking that she seemed so sweet.

As we set up the studio equipment for the photo shoot, Cheryl filled me in on everything she knew about her dog's past. Taffy had been used as a breeding dog in a commercial puppy mill for 7.5 to 8 years. Unlike puppies that are taken away from the mill to be sold to pet stores or sold online, breeding dogs (or "breeder dogs") are those dogs that remain at the mill to birth as many puppies as possible so that the mill owners can make as much money as possible. Kept in an outdoor wire-floor cage her whole life, like most breeder dogs, Taffy was overbred, so much so that when she was spayed her uterus broke apart in the veterinarian's hands. Because she lived in an outdoor cage and was constantly bred, she had deformed rear hips and rear legs and arthritis. Her teeth and gums were in such bad shape from severe periodontal disease that she needed to have seven teeth pulled. When she was no longer able to have as many puppies as was deemed profitable, she was dumped off at a local shelter, where she would have been euthanized if she hadn't been rescued by Ratbone Rescues. (Not many people are looking to adopt 8-year-old dogs with health issues.) Cheryl found out about Taffy, heard her story and knew she had to give Taffy the life she had always deserved. It wasn't easy at first. Having lived her entire life in an outdoor cage, Taffy now had to learn how to live in a house as a family pet. She was fearful of strangers, but over time she learned to associate people with fun. Her entire story saddened me, but I was really affected when I heard that at first, Taffy didn't know how to play. She had to learn what toys were. The mill had tattooed numbers and letters inside her ears to identify her. Up until she was rescued, she had never even had a name.

Looking at little Taffy run from Cheryl to Margie and back again to get affection and attention, and seeing her interact and play with Aka and with us—strangers in her home—was beyond moving. This little dog and her story touched me so much that I decided to create this book to raise awareness about dogs like Taffy—for those who had been rescued but also for the hundreds of thousands who are still suffering in puppy mills today. Cheryl tells Taffy's story to every person who meets them. Taffy is such a warm and loving dog now that when people meet her, they don't believe she lived in a puppy mill for almost 8 years. If you ever doubt that you can influence others with the decisions and choices you make in your life, then think about Taffy and all the people this little dog is influencing because she was so brave as to forget her past and begin to trust again. Maybe the people who meet her will be moved to act when they hear her story? Maybe they will act by NOT getting their next dog from a pet store or maybe they might influence their friends and family? Maybe they will choose to adopt or to volunteer with a rescue that saves puppy-mill dogs? Maybe they will get a group together to picket a local pet store that sells puppies, or maybe they will write to their congressman? Never doubt your ability (or one little dog's ability!) to influence people for the better.

WHAT IS A PUPPY MILL?

Puppy mills are inhumane commercial dog-breeding facilities that seek to minimize overhead costs in order to maximize profit. The health and welfare of the dogs are of no concern.

What are breeder dogs?

Unlike the puppies who are taken from the mill at a young age to be sold in pet stores and online, puppy-mill breeder dogs are the ones who are left behind to breed as many dogs as they possibly can. They spend their entire lives at the mill. When they are no longer able to produce enough puppies as is considered profitable, they are disposed of.

How are the dogs treated in the mills?

The mill owners decrease their operating expenses by maximizing their space, cutting the costs of the dog's medical care and food, and minimizing the amount of time necessary for people to clean, care and interact with the dogs.

As a result, life for most mill dogs is the same:

- **They live in stacked, wire-floor cages.** The cages have a wire floor so that the dogs don't need to be walked. Instead, they urinate and defecate in their crates, and because the crates are stacked, the dogs in the bottom crates must endure urine and feces "raining down" on them from above. This situation, and the fact that the dogs are often forced to lie in their own waste, causes skin irritations and burns. Dogs also often cut or even maim themselves when their feet get caught in the wire flooring. It is not uncommon for them to lose a paw or leg this way. Their pads and paws are usually cut from standing on the wire.

- **They live outside year-round.** The dogs are kept in outdoor housing or in buildings that often have no heating or air conditioning. Dogs left outside all year long must endure the cold and snow of winter and the heat of summer. The wire floors burn the dogs in the summertime. Dogs can easily die from exposure to the freezing cold or scorching heat.

- **They get no exercise.** Many dogs have never walked on grass or spent time outside of their crates. Some dogs don't even know how to walk. Walking on a floor or on the ground is a new and strange experience for them.

- **They get little to no medical care and are not groomed.** Puppy-mill dogs are usually suffering from untreated medical conditions, including genetic/hereditary diseases, tumors, periodontal disease, malnutrition, eye issues, skin infections and burns, torn pads, and infestations from internal and external parasites, including heartworm, Giardia and fleas. The lack of bathing and grooming creates matted fur, which causes pain and sores.

- **They are not socialized.** The dogs know little outside of the daily hell they experience in their crates. They are never given affection. They have no bedding to sleep on at night. They have never seen a toy and don't know how to play. They have little mental stimulation. Their day-to-day life is one of boredom and suffering.

- **Their food is poor quality.** Often puppy-mill dogs are fed the sweepings from the floor of the pet-food factories. This food is so low in nutritional value that the dogs often suffer malnutrition and begin losing their teeth and hair as a result.

- **They are overbred.** Female dogs are bred every heat cycle (typically twice per year) and as a result they suffer from permanent injuries, tumors and pain.

- **Some dogs are debarked.** If a dog is debarked, it is common for the operators to do so by ramming a pipe down the dog's throat.

- **They are used and then disposed of.** Breeder dogs are bred until they are no longer able to produce enough puppies as is deemed profitable. At that time, they are then disposed of. Those who are lucky enough to live (many are killed by being hit over the head or shot) are taken to auctions where they are sold to other mill operators or dropped off at kill shelters where they are likely to be euthanized since they are older, unsocialized and suffering from medical issues. A few operators will contact rescues to take the dogs they no longer want.

Where are puppy mills located?
Puppy mills are found all over the U.S., but mainly in the Midwest, with the highest concentration in Missouri; Upstate New York; and Lancaster County, Pennsylvania, where some members of the Amish and Mennonite communities breed dogs. The annual revenue from puppy mills in Lancaster County alone is estimated at $4 million. The ASPCA estimates there could be as many as 10,000 puppy mills in the U.S.

HOW DO THE BREEDER DOGS FARE AFTER THEY ARE RESCUED?
Every dog is an individual and reacts to his experiences in his own way. Typically, however, most mill dogs are shut down and scared of people at first but warm up to people over time. They need to learn how to play. Most have never lived outside of their crates, so they need to become socialized to everything—stairs and flooring, new people, unfamiliar noises, other dogs and animals, life in a home, life outside a home, etc. Most are not housebroken, which can be difficult for them to learn since these dogs are accustomed to urinating and defecating inside their own crates. Most have medical issues, diseases or infestations that need to be treated after they are rescued. Adopters find that all puppy-mill dogs need love, understanding and, above all, patience,

since the rehabilitation process can be slow. The little "wins" seem like huge victories—the first time the dog plays, approaches strangers, sits in their laps or climbs the stairs. For most adoptive families, rehabilitating and caring for a former puppy-mill breeder dog is a life-altering experience.

ARE PUPPY MILLS LEGAL?

Puppy-mill dogs are considered a commodity. They are a cash crop. The federal Animal Welfare Act (AWA) outlines minimum standards of care for dogs bred for commercial resale. The AWA requires breeders who have more than three breeding female dogs and who sell puppies to pet stores or brokers to be licensed and inspected by the U.S. Department of Agriculture (USDA). In addition, some states also have laws that regulate commercial breeding. Breeders who sell directly to the public, including through online sales, are not required to adhere to the AWA, although a new USDA rule has helped change this.

In most cases, however, the standards that breeders are required to meet are minimal. Under the AWA, it is completely legal to keep a dog for his entire life in a cage only six inches longer than his body in each direction, with a wire floor, stacked on top of another cage. These are conditions that most people would consider cruel and inhumane; however, they are completely legal. In addition, the Humane Society of the United States (HSUS) obtained inspection records that show many USDA-licensed breeders "getting away with" (i.e., rarely fined and without their licenses getting revoked) repeated violations of the already low standards of the AWA. To worsen the matter, the USDA employs only a small number of people to inspect thousands of puppy mills, research facilities, kennels and zoos.

CAN THE LAWS CHANGE?

While laws are slowly being implemented to help change the commercial dog-breeding industry, changes are few and far between. There are many large lobbying groups that do their best to keep these laws from being passed.

Change, however, is not impossible. Other countries are succeeding. In 2012, Ireland, which was once Europe's main supplier of puppies, implemented new laws to protect dogs in commercial-breeding facilities, including requirements to exercise the dogs, keep them in clean housing that is not overcrowded, and provide bedding, fresh food and water for the dogs. The law gives local veterinarians the right to inspect all facilities and the authority to shut down any facility that is failing to provide adequate care for its dogs. Vets can also monitor females to ensure they have only one litter of puppies per year. In addition, all breeders must be registered, and all puppies must be microchipped so they can be traced back to a specific breeder in the event of a problem. Harsh penalties are to be imposed on any breeder who does not comply with the new laws.

WHAT CAN WE DO TO STOP PUPPY MILLS?

While we can definitely write our congressmen and ask for stricter laws, a quicker way to help is to simply stop the demand for these dogs. The mill owners make most of their money through selling the dogs directly to pet stores or to brokers who sell them to pet stores, or by selling the dogs directly to the public, mostly online. By refusing to buy a dog from a pet store or off the Internet, we are eliminating the mill owners' platform for selling these dogs to the public, and therefore, their means of making money off these dogs. In other words, the best way to help is the following:

NEVER BUY A DOG FROM A PET STORE OR OFF THE INTERNET!

But my local pet store says its puppies aren't from a puppy mill!

Don't believe it! In the U.S., 99 percent of dogs sold in pet stores are from puppy mills. In addition to not wanting to support the mills, the public should not want to buy pet-store puppies because these dogs aren't healthy. A recent California study found that close to 50 percent of all puppies sold in pet stores were sick or incubating an illness. Nearly all pet-store puppies have parasites. In addition, many papers for pet-store puppies are fake. Most of these dogs are inbred and as a result might have genetic and/or psychological issues. It is important to stress that by buying a puppy from a pet store, you are not saving the life of a puppy-mill dog. You are supporting the business model that is keeping the mills profitable, and you are helping to put money into the pockets of the people who own these mills. You are condemning the parents of your puppy to lives filled with loneliness, misery and suffering.

Then what are the best options for getting my next dog?

It is my hope that people would consider adoption as their first choice. The HSUS estimates that approximately 3 to 4 million dogs and cats are euthanized in U.S. shelters annually. Despite lingering misconceptions and stereotypes, most shelter dogs are not damaged. As a former shelter volunteer, I met everything from a beautiful purebred Border Collie who was trained in agility to gorgeous newborn Labrador Retriever puppies. According to the National Council on Pet Population Study and Policy (NCPPSP), the number one reason that dogs are relinquished to shelters is because their owners are moving. In fact, nine out of the top 10 reasons have nothing to do with the dog's behavior but instead are problems the owner is having—job loss, divorce, allergies, etc.

What if I am looking for a specific breed?

If you think you cannot find a certain breed in a rescue or shelter, then guess again. Approximately 25 to 33 percent of dogs in shelters are purebreds. In addition, all across the country, there are breed-specific rescues for every breed there is. These rescues are run by loving, caring individuals and foster-home volunteers who are just as passionate about the breed and the care of these dogs as you are. I have met volunteers from many of these groups in person, and I cannot say enough nice things about them.

But I must get a dog from a breeder!

If you feel you must buy a dog from a breeder, then please make sure you get a dog from a breeder you have met. Responsible breeders do NOT sell dogs to pet stores. Responsible breeders will have no problem with you coming to meet them, the parents (or at least the mother) of the puppies you are interested in, or the facilities or home the dogs are in. They will be happy to meet you because they want to ensure their dogs are going to good homes. They take care and pride in the dogs they produce and do not overbreed their dogs.

Other ways to help

Puppy mills add to the dog overpopulation problem. Help control the pet population, and as a result, the number of dogs euthanized in shelters each year:

Get your dogs and cats spayed and neutered.

THIS PROJECT & THE DOGS IN THIS BOOK

All the dogs in this book have been lucky enough to find their forever homes, and I feel honored to have met them and the caring people who took them in as members of their families. Some of these dogs were taken from mills when they were young; others were taken when they were old. Some are from big mills and others from small "backyard breeders." Some have had easy rehabilitations, and others have had a hard time adjusting to life in a home, and learning to trust new people and to feel safe in new environments. Every dog is different, and every puppy-mill dog is an individual who is learning to get through the day the best way he or she knows how. While Taffy and her story affected me and caused me to act by creating this book to help educate others about puppy mills, I am hoping the dogs in this book and their stories will have a similar effect on you. Hopefully, we can all spread the word about puppy mills and do our best to educate others so that those we know and love don't unknowingly contribute to the problem by purchasing a puppy from a pet store or online.

For more information on puppy mills, please refer to the Puppy-Mill Facts & Resources sections (see pgs. 104 & 105). The facts in the introduction of this book were taken from the HSUS and ASPCA websites.

PUPPY-MILL
SURVIVORS

In the dogs' biographies: If a dog lives with another dog who did not come from the same litter, the dog is referred to in quotation marks as the dog's "sister," "brother" or "sibling." If the dogs are actual littermates or blood relatives, then there are no quotation marks around mother, sister, brother, etc. Only the participants' first names are used; their surnames have been omitted. Quotations in a dog's biography are the words of the dog's "person/people" unless otherwise noted.

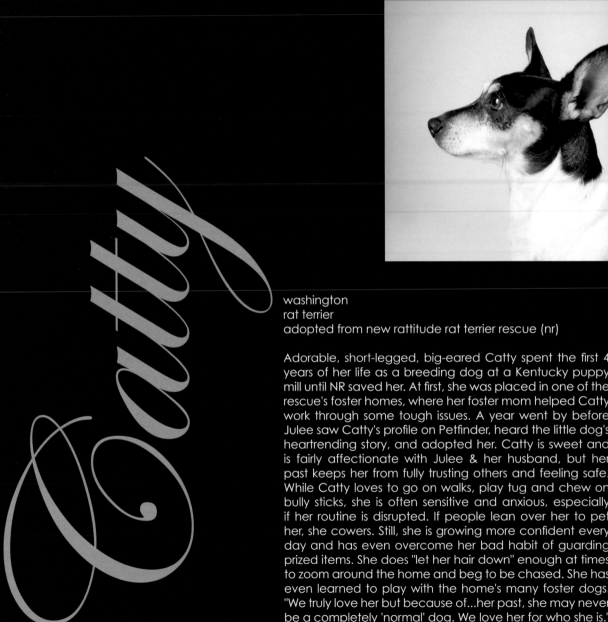

Catty

washington
rat terrier
adopted from new rattitude rat terrier rescue (nr)

Adorable, short-legged, big-eared Catty spent the first 4 years of her life as a breeding dog at a Kentucky puppy mill until NR saved her. At first, she was placed in one of the rescue's foster homes, where her foster mom helped Catty work through some tough issues. A year went by before Julee saw Catty's profile on Petfinder, heard the little dog's heartrending story, and adopted her. Catty is sweet and is fairly affectionate with Julee & her husband, but her past keeps her from fully trusting others and feeling safe. While Catty loves to go on walks, play tug and chew on bully sticks, she is often sensitive and anxious, especially if her routine is disrupted. If people lean over her to pet her, she cowers. Still, she is growing more confident every day and has even overcome her bad habit of guarding prized items. She does "let her hair down" enough at times to zoom around the home and beg to be chased. She has even learned to play with the home's many foster dogs. "We truly love her but because of...her past, she may never be a completely 'normal' dog. We love her for who she is."

alabama
miniature long-haired dachshund
adopted from greater birmingham humane society (gbhs)

Pulled from an Alabama puppy mill that was packed with over 200 dogs, Penny was emaciated and full of worms. Penny and many others were taken to GBHS where they got medical attention. Penny had many issues, including a life-threatening heart condition for which she needed an operation. Her hair was so matted that it fell out. At the mill, the dogs were housed in stacked wire crates. As a result of her crate being below others, Penny had burns and permanent hair loss on her back from years of dog urine and feces "raining down" on her. She also has chronic dry eyes that need daily drops. Very shy, Penny slowly warmed to the volunteers who were helping to socialize the mill dogs. Laurie, one of the volunteers, got Penny the surgery she needed and adopted her. Penny, who is now expected to live a normal life, has been by Laurie's side ever since. She fits in with the home's other pets and loves snuggling, hiking, chasing birds and taking her Nose Work classes, where she is learning to be around strangers. "I love Penny with all my heart and will do everything to ensure that the rest of her life is filled with joy, comfort and fun!"

"Puppy-mill dogs have had little to no positive contact with people....I would tell people considering adopting a rescued mill dog to be consistent and even-tempered around the dog. Allow the dog to open up to you and learn to trust....If you do that then you will get to experience not only the unconditional love of a pet but the amazing transformation that takes place when an abused animal learns to give that love."

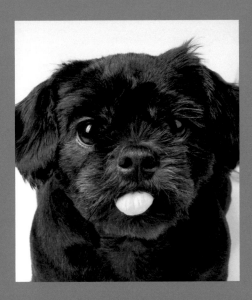

new york
shih tzu
adopted from north shore animal league america (nsala)

Wicket was born in a Missouri puppy mill, sold to a pet store, bought by a customer, returned to the store, and then sent back to the mill—all before he was 8 months old. He was soon rescued and arrived at NSALA, where employee Gregory was there to carry him off the truck. They bonded instantly. At the shelter, Wicket's medical issues, including stomach parasites and severe ear infections, made him cranky, but every time Gregory would walk past his crate, Wicket would stretch out his paw to play. Gregory fostered Wicket in hopes of increasing the dog's chances of getting adopted. Wicket and Gregory's other dog, Gus, got along immediately, and Wicket quickly bonded with Gregory's mother. Although Wicket has mental scars from his past, he continues to make real progress. He loves playing, especially with people, and is always up to something, often trying to get his pal Gus to participate in his mischief. He has become Gus's shadow, following him around and trying to imitate him. Wicket continues to surprise Gregory with just how much he is improving and with what a great addition to the household he is since they adopted him.

Emily | 23

louisiana
whippet
adopted from whippet rescue and placement (wrap)

In 2008, animal control officers raided a property and seized dogs from some of the worst conditions they had ever seen. The dogs, kept in outdoor wire cages that were barely bigger than they were, had never been let out, and some dogs did not know how to walk. Many were lying in dirt and feces. They were infested with practically everything, including heartworm. Having emerged from these conditions with a warm, trusting, social personality, which she had from Day 1 of being rescued, Emily is nothing short of a miracle. As soon as Jenny & Yvonne met her, they knew she was to be theirs. At first, despite being several years old, Emily had the enthusiasm and social graces of a puppy; luckily, the home's other Whippet, Blaze, was tolerant of her new "sister's" behavior. Emily loves her new family and is now a happy social butterfly whom most people in the neighborhood know by name. She must feel she is the luckiest dog in the world to have found such a wonderful, caring family, including attentive grandparents who spoil her and a loving older "sister" to keep her from ever feeling alone again.

virginia
schnauzer - poodle mix (schnoodle)
adopted from north shore animal league america (nsala)

For nearly 5 years, Macy was a breeder dog, kept in a tiny cage with another dog at an Oklahoma puppy mill, where she was known simply as "#13," as the tattoo in her ear denotes. Luckily, she was rescued and taken to NSALA. And, it was on Thanksgiving Day that Irene's son, a NSALA veterinarian, called to let her know he had the perfect dog for her. When they met, Macy stole Irene's heart. They named her "Macy" after the parade. Initially, Macy could not navigate stairs, was not housebroken, was scared to walk outside and would shake whenever anyone came near her. She quickly overcame those fears. She has gained so much confidence that people are now shocked when they find out she is a former mill dog. Today, Macy is a happy little dog, and she adjusts easily to new places. She does have minor vision issues, but it does not slow her down. Macy loves snuggling on Irene's lap at night while Irene watches TV, being with Irene's daughter and grandchildren, and going for walks. Irene is so grateful to her son for bringing Macy into her life. "It seems as if she's been here forever!"

"I'm convinced that he knows the difference between this life and the one he knew before, and I can see the gratitude in his big brown eyes. He is my little old man, and he has amazing spirit despite the bumpy road he has traveled."

Stanley, thoroughly enjoying a jar of peanut butter that he "stole" from the photographer during his photo shoot

connecticut
dachshund
adopted from meriden humane society (mhs)

Stanley was dropped off at MHS by an alleged mill owner who periodically relinquishes breeder dogs she no longer wants to the shelter. There, 10-year-old Stanley, extremely shy, scared and closed off, waited for his forever home. As soon as Rebecca met him, she knew she had to adopt him and give him the good home he always deserved. However, the first few months were tough. His mouth was abscessed, but the vet managed to save a few teeth, including his two top canine teeth, which left him looking like an adorable vampire. A change in diet soon improved the poor state of his coat and skin. At first, he did not understand what "outside" was, and when inside, he would sit on top of the coffee table and shiver. He trusted Rebecca right away, and through exposure, he slowly began to trust others. Canine "brother" Wally taught him friendship and how to play. Rebecca taught him that he deserved to be loved. He soon became a totally different dog. He now loves to snuggle, to go for walks and car rides, and to visit Grandma's house. Remarkably, within a year, he triumphed over his past. He has no remaining issues.

indiana
beagle - rat terrier mix
adopted from animal control in richmond, indiana

Born in a puppy mill, Baby was the only pup from her litter to survive. The mill owners still intended to breed her despite her being paralyzed from the waist down. She was marked with a cattle tag, which left a dime-sized hole in her ear. It is unclear how she was rescued, but she came to live with an elderly woman who, before long, could no longer care for her. The woman's landlord called animal control, and after seeing what a lovebug Baby was, the staff could not put her down. No one stepped up to take her until Jessica & Chris found out about her and adopted her. She adapted well to her new home. At the time she was photographed, Baby was one of 10 dogs in the house (4 were paralyzed). Baby requires a little more care than most dogs. She wears baby overalls and a diaper that needs to be changed several times a day, and she often utilizes a wheelchair or a stroller to get around. People are curious about her and give her lots of sympathy. Baby doesn't feel sorry for herself though; she is a happy little girl who loves everyone and seems to realize the great chance she was given with her new family, who spoil and love her greatly.

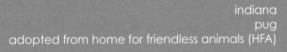

indiana
pug
adopted from home for friendless animals (HFA)

When Jessica's (*see pg. 34*) beloved Rat Terrier, Patch, passed away, her son Tyler asked whether they could adopt a Pug, and so they went to HFA to adopt a 9-year-old Pug. They couldn't decide on a name for her. When they adopted her, her name at the shelter was the same as one of their other dogs, so they couldn't use that name. Over time, they started to call her Pug, and it stuck. They know little about Pug's history except that she was from a puppy mill and had birthed numerous litters. Because of her age and history, she was accustomed to going to the bathroom in her crate, so housebreaking her proved difficult. In addition, her rear leg has a luxating patella, which causes her to sit in a strange way. Otherwise, despite her past, she is a remarkably well-adjusted, friendly girl who adores people, especially Tyler; she follows him around like she is his shadow. Tyler, who has autism, needs her, too. Whenever Tyler feels anxious or upset, he turns to Pug. She calms him down; it is as if she knows he needs comforting. Pug likes to play and explore, but mostly she just enjoys being with Tyler.

new york
bichon frise - poodle mix
adopted from north shore animal league america (nsala)

Jennifer had just started working at NSALA when 3-year-old Teddy was brought in with other mill dogs from Missouri. Jennifer thought cute Teddy would get adopted right away, but when he was still there a month later (looked over repeatedly due to his bad psychological state), she knew she had to adopt him. However, many people wondered why she did. For the first 3 months, he would not even look at her. He just sat in the back of his crate, hung his head, and looked sad. He did not leave his crate for the first 8 months. Everything petrified him. He would shudder when Jennifer touched him. Her heart broke for him, but she knew he had it in him to get better. And then, after 9 months, Teddy ran out of his crate and never looked back. He is still scared of new people, but he has relaxed around Jennifer's friends and family. Now an affectionate and cuddly dog who enjoys life, he often rolls on his back to get belly rubs and loves romping with his canine "sister." "The greatest joy in my life...has been watching Teddy blossom into the amazing, happy, spunky dog that I always knew he could be."

Miley

new york
cavalier king charles spaniel
adopted from north shore animal league america (nsala)

Miley spent the first 6 months of her life in the deplorable conditions of a Midwest puppy mill until she was rescued and brought to NSALA. Soon afterward, Matthew & Susan adopted her. At first, Miley needed extra TLC. She had to know that she was in a home where she was safe and loved. She eventually came out of her shell. She did not bark for the first 2 months they had her, but now she communicates all of the time. Susan likes to say they helped Miley "find her true voice." The only remaining issue is her fear of loud noises. Miley is much more confident and is living the good life with lots of love and attention from Matthew, Susan and their two daughters. Every time Miley enters the house, she makes sure to find her best friend—the family cat, Belding. They love to play and nap together. Miley loves all dogs and people, and she greets strangers as if she has known them her whole life. A number of people have adopted from a shelter after meeting little Miley. The family knows Miley appreciates her new life with them, and they all also feel truly lucky to have found her.

new york
shih tzu mix
adopted from north shore animal league america (nsala)

Born in a puppy mill in Colorado, Calli was saved when she was just 4 months old and brought to NSALA in New York. Bruce, a volunteer at NSALA, was assisting in bringing the rescued animals inside from the mobile units when Calli, who was in a cage with a sibling, caught his attention. He adopted her shortly afterward. Since then, adorable Calli has become a star attraction at his apartment building with everyone from little children to adults. Calli adores people and is especially friendly with the female senior citizens in the park across from Bruce's apartment. She has a spot on a favorite park bench where she likes to greet her "public" and watch the world go by. People often say how calm, cute and friendly she is. Calli's many loves include eating cheese snacks, watching TV, riding in the car and playing with the cat's toys. She likes to stand on her hind legs unattended for as long as she can. She has been socialized with all kinds of dogs—from Chihuahuas to Chows. Calli enjoys a very peaceful and loving coexistence with Bruce's elderly cat. "She is the best friend anyone could have."

new york
a breed test confirmed she is 100% staffordshire bull terrier
adopted from previous "owners"

A couple looking to rehome a pit bull approached Julie at a gas station. Julie took one look at Cuda and knew she had to take her. She & her husband, Scott, know nothing about Cuda's past except that the couple, feeling sorry for Cuda, had purchased her for $50 from a breeder on Craigslist. Cuda has physical traits that may be associated with inbreeding, including cow-hocked rear legs, an undersized body, a massive underbite, a curved spine, fused vertebrae, asymmetrical ears, an enlarged heart, an underdeveloped pancreas and diabetes. She is in no pain, but she visits the vet twice monthly. Cuda attends events to educate people about backyard and irresponsible breeders. She helps raise money for rescues, educates people about pit bulls and teaches children about accepting others as they are. Julie & Scott helped create "Cuda Cares," which focuses on education and breeder regulations. When people see Cuda for the first time, they have stunned expressions that turn into broad smiles. She steals the heart of everyone she meets.

Molly &

new hampshire
standard poodles
adopted from rolling dog farm (rdf)

Molly and Priscilla, two blind poodle sisters, were brought in to an animal shelter in Texas from a puppy mill. They would have been euthanized if a local woman hadn't worked very hard to save them. She picked them up, and, even though she had bathed them once, they stank so badly of urine that she could barely breathe with them in her car. The woman suspected that the puppy mill where they had come from had just kept them in cages and let their urine and feces pile up until it saturated their coats and skin. They must have been lying in their own waste. They were horribly matted and filthy, had infected ears and kennel cough and were about 15 lbs. underweight each. Despite their state, they were docile and very happy to be out. The woman didn't think they had ever been on grass before. She contacted a local rescue, which in turn contacted RDF, a rescue that takes in dogs with disabilities (with a soft spot for blind dogs). Very long story short (it often takes a village to rescue dogs!), teamwork between the woman, the rescue and RDF eventually got the sisters to Montana, • • • • • • • • •

where RDF was located at the time. RDF took great care of them. The duo was sweet but a little shy at first. They turned into real Montana "ranch dogs" who loved roaming the fenced-in yards with the rescue's other dogs. They made friends with a hound dog named Trooper and used him as their "eyes." The girls remained at the rescue for 3 years, and it was only after RDF moved to New Hampshire that the sisters were brought to the attention of Kat & Kris, who eventually adopted them. The girls are now living in "doggy paradise" in the New Hampshire countryside with lots of space and in a home that truly loves and appreciates them. Their "sibling" Franky, a Dachshund, is their good friend, partner in crime and playmate (they even manage to play three-way tug of war together). Now, similar to Trooper at RDF, he acts as the girls' "eyes" as they follow him around from place to place. Together they are "The Three Musketeers." Both dogs love people and can be submissive around other dogs. They respond well to Kat's voice and know the house and the routine—when they go for a walk, when they go to bed or when it is feeding time. They are both affectionate and love their walks. Everyone who meets them adores them since they are so friendly. It was years in the making, but they are so fortunate to have at last found the forever home they always dreamed of.

Priscilla

"He lights up any room he is in, and any person who comes in contact with him falls in love with him.... He is very loving and happy.... He loves anyone and everyone."

illinois
miniature long-haired dachshund
adopted from midwest dachshund rescue (mwdr)

Henry's breeder bred dapple (merle) Dachshunds together to try to make white Dachshunds; however, merle dogs should never be bred together because the litters produce "double merles" (or "double dapples," which is what Henry is). Double merles have vision/eye problems and/or deafness. Henry was born deaf (he may be able to hear some noises) and with just one eye, through which, because it is underdeveloped, he has limited vision. Henry's limitations in no way impede him from living a normal, happy life. However, as is the fate of many double merles, Henry was relinquished to a shelter because of his shortcomings. He might have been put down had it not been for MWDR. At 8 months old, Henry was adopted by Spencer & his family, who already had another miniature Dachshund named Harriet. She and Henry hit it off immediately. Today, they are inseparable. Henry relies on Harriet to get around and to find his way when adventuring. Harriet will even retrieve him when it is time to come in. Henry is a joy who will "sit on your lap and make your day instantly better." His family thinks he will make a great therapy dog one day. He has brightened up their lives, and they feel very lucky to have him. He could not be more loved.

new york
japanese chin - tibetan spaniel mix
adopted from north shore animal league america (nsala)

Jayne (*see pg. 61*), who works at NSALA, was there the day 6-month-old Turtle arrived at the shelter after being rescued from a Missouri puppy mill. At the time, Jayne's Japanese Chin, Bonsai, was ill; she was in no frame of mind to get another dog. However, every time she walked by Turtle's cage, he would reach out to her and cry. She would open his cage, and he would hug her like a person. She took him back to her office to meet Bonsai, and Turtle rested next to Bonsai to comfort him. Jayne fostered Turtle and knew he was hers to keep. They both grieved terribly when Bonsai later passed away. Today, Turtle adores Jayne, whom he follows around like a shadow. He has a favorite teddy bear that he carries around with him. When he naps, he uses the bear as a pillow. Clever Turtle can also open drawers, doors and childproof caps, so Jayne has to lock cabinets as a result. He loves empty plastic water bottles, and he stashes every can and plastic bottle he can find in his toy tent (aka his "man cave"). "He has to be the sweetest dog I ever met....Turtle adopted me. It was the best thing that ever happened."

new york
shih tzu - miniature poodle mix
adopted from north shore animal league america (nsala)

Missouri puppy-mill dog Simba was briefly adopted by a woman, but it wasn't long before she, for reasons unknown, turned Simba and her other dog, a Labrador Retriever, over to a rescue. By chance, they wound up on a truck full of rescued puppy-mill dogs bound for NSALA. It was there that Jayne (*see pg. 60*) first saw 6-month-old Simba. Jayne adopted Simba exactly 1 year after her other dog, Turtle. While Turtle is sweet and gentle, Simba has more of a bad-boy/devil-may-care attitude. Simba is good with people and everyone loves him, but his real love is other dogs, especially Turtle. He often pesters Turtle for attention, and kind Turtle tolerates his behavior. Simba has a toy tent like Turtle's, but he prefers to be in Turtle's tent. Turtle, on the other hand, really likes his time alone! As it turns out, both of Jayne's dogs are hoarders: Turtle stashes away bottles and cans in his tent, and tiny, 6-lb. Simba picks up pine cones outside that are bigger than he is and brings them home to hide in his bed. Jayne loves her dogs and describes rescuing puppy-mill dogs as being "one of the greatest joys a human being can experience."

"The Indiana 15" & "The Band of Brothers"

In 2011, New Rattitude (NR) got word that a breeder was releasing 15 Rat Terriers—all 3 to 4 months old, mostly males. They were told if the dogs were not rescued, they would be killed. NR replied right away that it would help. The breeder was a legal, licensed commercial operator, and these puppies were "overstock." The operator had bred more puppies than he could sell in the narrow window during which a puppy is considered marketable, and now the puppies were nothing more than worthless "inventory." Without rescue intervention, overstock pups like these are typically killed. The mill also had too many puppies to stay in compliance with its state license. At the mill, they had been kept in rabbit hutches with many pups to a pen. When they came to NR, the dogs reeked and had loose, bloody stools likely from a parasitic infestation. Otherwise, they were in good health...or so NR thought. The pups were sent to foster homes in various states. Four males (who came to be called "The Band of Brothers"), Alex, Jasper, Hoagie and Reuben, went to Washington state. Alex was delivered to first-time foster parents Cindy & Andrew, Jasper joined Julee & Brett (see pg. 14), and Reuben and Hoagie stayed with Janell. The "Indiana 15" had been saved. However, within 2 weeks of arriving at their foster homes, three of the 15 puppies had broken a leg, including Hoagie. There was no disputing that some nutritional and/or genetic deficiency was to blame. The rescue consulted vets, who blamed the broken bones on the pups' possible poor nutrition, lack of exercise and/or cramped conditions for all of their short lives. During the crucial stages of their development, when they needed nutrition and exercise to help their muscles develop to support their skeletal systems, the mill deprived the pups of both. All foster families were advised to confine the pups to a small room when indoors and to increase their exercise space gradually. They were also cautioned to keep the puppies off wood and tile floors and not to allow any jumping on or off furniture. The puppies' muscles, tendons and ligaments needed time to develop before the dogs could play as much and as rigorously as they wanted to. Fortunately, no more breaks occurred, and all 15 puppies continued to thrive and become healthy and strong. NR's vet bills for the broken legs totaled over $1,000. After the initial health concerns, socialization and potty training were the two biggest challenges for the pups. They were all 3 to 4 months old and, like most mill dogs, they received very little human interaction during their time at the mill. Even the experienced NR foster families who had fostered many mill dogs in the past agreed that these puppies were more fearful than most. When the puppies first arrived at their foster homes, they were scared to death of humans and had no idea how to play. They showed no interest in toys. They were always on guard. It is unusual for young puppies to have such an intense fear of people. In addition, it took weeks to sort out their unhealthy digestive systems. Despite all the initial difficulties, it was a joy for the foster families to see the pups overcome their issues. Cindy, who had just joined the NR Washington team when the mill pups were rescued, found the experience of fostering Alex to be inspiring. "Taking Alex as my first foster and my first mill pup was both scary and exciting. Seeing him come out of his crate for the first time and how scared he was and unsure of his surroundings broke my heart." Janell had the difficulty of rehabilitating both Reuben and Hoagie, while ensuring Hoagie's broken leg was able to heal. As for Jasper, he had a longer road to recovery. While Jasper was in good physical health, psychologically he was damaged. Jasper displayed some separation distress while he was with Julee & Brett. However, once he was adopted, it turned into full-blown severe separation anxiety, and he had to be returned to NR. It is possible little Jasper's anxiety was caused by inbreeding, which can cause psychological as well as physiological problems. Luckily for Jasper, one of NR's retired foster parents adopted him, so he is never left alone for more than a couple of hours a week. With this home life, he is a happy-go-lucky boy whose anxiety has stabilized. All four of "The Band of Brothers" are now doing well and in loving homes.

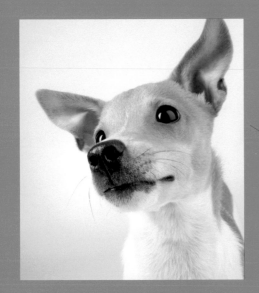

new jersey
miniature pinscher
adopted from internet miniature pinscher service (imps)

In 2001, IMPS received word that the state had shut down an Amish puppy mill in Lancaster, PA that contained over 1,000 dogs. A local shelter brought trucks and people to save as many dogs as they could since the man was literally throwing the dogs over his fence and was threatening to kill the dogs if no one took them. The shelter was packed with crates of small dogs that had been saved. Nancy, an IMPS member, helped to pick up four adult minpins and one mother with four 2-day-old puppies from the shelter. Nancy & her husband, Vince, fostered the mother and her pups, and because they arrived on Sept. 11, the couple called the pups Hope, Star, Liberty and Glory. Nancy & Vince adopted Glory, and the others all found good homes. Despite being socialized, the pups are scared of strangers. Glory still hides when new people are in the house. Otherwise, she is a happy dog whose nickname is "Wiggle Butt." She prefers dogs to people, which is good since Nancy & Vince have fostered hundreds of dogs and at one point had nine minpins of their own. Active in IMPS for over 14 years, Nancy & Vince always try to educate people about puppy mills. "We can only hope that we have enlightened at least a few people during that time."

new york
french bulldog
adopted from north shore animal league america (nsala)

After 5 years of being used as a breeding dog and having had multiple litters, Dumpling was rescued from the terrible conditions of an Oklahoma puppy mill and brought to NSALA. While under anesthesia to get spayed, Dumpling had several embedded pebbles removed from in-between the pads of her feet. She has scars on her front legs. Her most defining characteristic is her abnormal gait: she hops on her front legs like a bunny instead of extending her legs normally when she runs. She was placed in a foster home, but Dianne, who works at NSALA, had already fallen in love with her. Dumpling adjusted well to life in her new home with Dianne, her husband (Kevin), their daughters (Michelle & Brianne), a Lab and two cats. Dumpling is good with people and other dogs but is still afraid of brooms. She was easy to housebreak despite having lived in a cage her whole life. While her X-rays showed poor conformation of her front legs, she still lives a normal active life like any other dog. She likes to run, catch balls and play tug of war. And, when the mood strikes her, she will run laps around the yard or living room to revel in her newfound freedom.

"Puppy-mill dogs need patient, dedicated owners, but the rewards of seeing your mill dog become a happy, well-adjusted family member cannot be understated. They reward you with immeasurable love and loyalty."

new york
cavalier king charles spaniel
adopted from north shore animal league america (nsala)

Grace was saved from a commercial puppy mill in the Midwest when she was almost 3 years old. Grace and 54 other small dogs arrived at NSALA, where Pat first met and adopted her. While Grace quickly bonded with Pat, it took her some time to trust others. It was a year before she would approach people, but sweet Grace has blossomed in the 2 years she has been with Pat's family, and now she will even approach strangers. She loves to go to work with Pat and make the rounds to get treats and attention. She is a lapdog who loves a good nap. Cavaliers are "typically" merry and outgoing, but Grace takes life seriously. She can, however, be mischievous, like when she shreds the mail. Once, patrolling the yard to keep out intruders, this 15-lb. girl treed a raccoon, which gave Pat a scare, but Grace was very pleased with herself! Adopting her was so rewarding for Pat that she has since adopted two more mill dogs (see pgs. 80 & 81), whom Grace loves to play with. From them Pat has learned that "every dog is an individual and mill dogs are no different. Some just need more time and patience to overcome their past." Pat always makes sure to educate people about puppy mills and puppy-mill dogs wherever they go.

Hayley

new york
cavalier king charles spaniel
adopted from north shore animal league america (nsala)

In 2010, Hayley was rescued from a Midwest puppy mill where she had been used as a breeding dog for over 7 years. Hayley has mitral valve disease, a congenital heart condition that unfortunately she probably passed on to many of her offspring. It is clear the puppy mill that housed Hayley cared nothing about her health or the health of the puppies she produced; as long as she continued to produce litters, they could sell them and make a profit. Amazingly enough, Hayley came away virtually emotionally intact. She has a very even temperament. When Pat (*see pgs. 75 & 81*) first saw her at NSALA, unlike the other dogs from her rescue who were traumatized and fearful, Hayley was sitting at the front of her cage, wagging her tail and trying to catch someone's attention. Hayley quickly adapted to life as a family member in a home. She now lives in a house with a big backyard. Two of her dog "sisters" are mill rescues, as well. Hayley is a testament to the resilience a dog can show even coming from the worst conditions. Her sweet nature and love of life come through in everything she does; her happiness is contagious. Hayley is truly an ambassador for all shelter and puppy-mill dogs.

new york
cavalier king charles spaniel
adopted from cavalier rescue usa (cr)

Born in a Colorado puppy mill, Maddy was held back when the rest of her litter was sold. The mill owner changed his mind when Maddy was around 5 months old. He decided that he already had enough breeding dogs of her breed and worked with CR on her release. She then went into a foster home. Pat (*see pgs. 75 & 80*) first heard about Maddy from a volunteer at National Mill Dog Rescue. It wasn't easy to arrange, but eventually Maddy boarded a Pet Airways plane and landed in New York. She was tired and confused from her trip, but she wagged her tail and licked Pat's hand. She was home at last! Luckily, Maddy has no issues from her past. She walked into Pat's home and inserted herself into the pack as if she had been there all along. There has never been a single squabble among the dogs. She and "sister" Grace are wrestling partners; they have a special bond and even have subtle ways of communicating. Maddy's sunny disposition is ever present. She loves everyone. Rarely walking, she prefers instead to take on life at full speed. She is a clown—always ready for some fun. Above all, Maddy loves to be cuddled and turns into a boneless puddle of fur during any neck or belly rub.

new jersey
boston terrier
rescued from a pet store

Approximately 99 percent of dogs sold in pet stores are from puppy mills. Their parents suffer in horrendous conditions, and it is those horrible conditions that these pups are born into. As a result, many of the dogs sold at these stores have genetic issues, parasites, or other illnesses that they contracted while still at the mills. Miss Pickles is a perfect example of the kind of neglect and disregard the mill owners have for the quality, well-being and health of the puppies they produce. Miss Pickles was born at a mill and put up for sale at a pet store. When Christine found her, Miss Pickles was already extremely sick. She knew that if she didn't take her, Miss Pickles would certainly die. Christine took her to a vet, who thought Miss Pickles wouldn't survive the night. Luckily, she pulled through. It was a week later that Christine discovered Miss Pickles was also deaf. Now completely healthy and as sweet and sour as her name suggests, Miss Pickles is happy playing fetch and ruling the roost at the home that she shares with three other dogs. Miss Pickles has been a "dream dog—the easiest dog to train."

new york
boston terrier mix
adopted from north shore animal league america (nsala)

When he was about 3 years old, Kogi was rescued from a Tennessee puppy mill where he was used for breeding. He had corneal scars in both eyes due to his keratoconjunctivitis sicca and purulent discharge. He had scabs between his eyes and two big scars by his shoulders, perhaps from an embedded harness. When Clara first saw him at NSALA, where she works, she felt an instant bond with him. She & her husband, Rodolfo, adopted him. Kogi still has a few issues from his past. He is wary of strangers (if he is approached too fast he cowers), but he is very gentle with people. He is also petrified of thunderstorms and fireworks. Despite everything, Kogi is a happy dog and has a great life now. His eyes are better. Each day, he gets at least two hour-long walks and is usually not left alone for more than 5 hours. He goes everywhere Clara & Rodolfo go. He is a real character, too. At the beach, he runs away from waves. He snorts like a pig and has a goofy grin from a few missing teeth. He will nap or cuddle anywhere, anytime. The couple shares Kogi's story with everyone who meets him to educate them about puppy mills and shelter dogs. "He has made our lives richer, and we cannot imagine living without him! We love him with all our hearts."

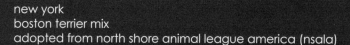

maryland
yorkshire terrier
adopted from washington animal rescue league (warl)

In 2009, the Humane Society (HSUS) raided an Arkansas property and found trailers filled with small, filthy cages stacked floor to ceiling that contained around 100 small dogs. Masks protected the rescuers from the pungent ammonia-filled air, caused by the dogs urinating and defecating in their wire-floored crates, which were stacked one atop another. The dogs were matted, emaciated and suffering from skin and eye infections, and other ailments. They likely had never known life outside their cramped enclosures. The dogs received medical care and grooming and were transported to WARL in DC. It was there that Layla, a breeder dog from the HSUS rescue, was adopted by Anne & Kelly. Initially, 5-year-old Layla had to start almost from scratch. She had to learn how to navigate stairs. She was not (and is still working on being) housebroken. She had never played. A month after they brought her home, she began to chew on and growl at a toy for the first time. "It was amazing!" It is the little victories that make rehabilitating a puppy-mill dog so rewarding. She now loves to play. Layla is good with other dogs and remains fearful of new people, but she is improving! "All adoptees need our patience, understanding, clear limits and tons of reinforcement and love."

new york
pekingese
adopted from north shore animal league america (nsala)

For 4 years, Sweet Pea was a breeder dog in a Missouri puppy mill. Her ears were so infected when she came to NSALA that she eventually needed surgery. She was also pregnant and gave birth to three pups that did not look Pekingese. After the pups stopped nursing, Marilyn, who had fostered many puppy-mill dogs in the past, took Sweet Pea in and soon adopted her. Marilyn's father had recently died and her mother, Marie, kept asking her to bring Sweet Pea over to visit. After a while, Marilyn left Sweet Pea at her mother's home to keep her company, and it wasn't long before the dog became very attached to Marie. Marie was recovering from a broken shoulder, and Sweet Pea gave her a purpose and motivated her to go outside and walk. Sweet Pea now goes with her anywhere dogs are welcomed. At home, she follows her from room to room. When Marie goes to the basement, Sweet Pea sits at the top of the stairs and waits for her to return. When her friends show each other photos of their grandchildren, Marie shares pictures of Sweet Pea. While she remains shy of people and fearful of men, Sweet Pea loves other dogs and children and has adjusted well to life with Marilyn & Marie. She loves them both very much. Sweet Pea is a princess in their eyes. She has no wants.

maryland
silky terrier
adopted from washington animal rescue league (warl)

In 2008, in what was the largest puppy-mill raid to date in Tennessee, the Humane Society (HSUS) rescued 700 dogs, all living outside in filthy wire-floor cages. Dead dogs were found. What food the dogs had was rotten. Many of the dogs had to be euthanized. Maggie, a breeding dog at the mill, was taken along with about 70 other dogs to WARL, where volunteers Stacey & Nick first saw "a little spark in her" and adopted her. At first, she was scared of everything—the sound of shoes hitting the pavement, cars, blowing leaves, birds, but mostly people—she would run away from Stacey & Nick with her tail tucked down and her ears back. They continued to work with her every day. Maggie went from avoiding contact with them, to tolerating it, to demanding it! Her progress has never plateaued; she continues to gain confidence and to try new things. It is a treat for the couple now to see her when she is totally relaxed, like when she naps in the sunshine. Maggie has helped the couple educate others about puppy mills. Their neighbors regularly comment on Maggie's amazing transformation. Some say that she seems bigger now, but she just appears that way since she has gained so much confidence. It has taken a lot of patience on Stacey & Nick's part, but the rewards for them have been great.

"Rookie has the best personality of any dog I've ever met or had. He makes us so happy.... We may be biased, but he's just the best pup in the world!"

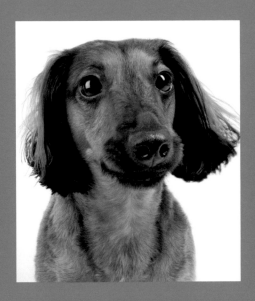

ohio
dachshund
adopted from all rover's rescue friends (arrf)

An 8-week-old male Dachshund and his littermates were rescued from a puppy mill before being medically treated and put up for adoption at ARRF. Winter & her husband, Derek, adopted the male pup and called him "Rookie" to give him a name that had a connection with Derek's work as a police officer. Fortunately, since he was saved from the mill at such a young age, Rookie has no issues to speak of. He has a little separation anxiety, but that may have less to do with his past and more to do with the fact that this lucky pup has constant company (Winter & Derek work opposite shifts, so someone is usually home). Rookie is a joy and an endless source of amusement: he loves to have staring contests with them; to hide (secretly) his chewy in the folds of the couch covers when they aren't looking; to hold his blankets or bed in his mouth for extended periods of time for no reason at all; and to sleep under the covers while laying his head on a pillow just like a person. Rookie adjusted extremely well when the couple's son, Dane, was born, too. Rookie loves Dane. He kisses him in the morning through the slats in the crib and follows around whoever is carrying him. It is as if Rookie is just making sure that the baby is OK. "We just love him to pieces!"

north carolina
rat terrier
adopted from ratbone rescues (rr)

Taffy spent the first 8 years of her life as a puppy-mill breeder dog. She has deformed hips and rear legs, and has since developed arthritis in these joints, from being constantly bred and from living in an outdoor wire-floor cage. Taffy needed to have seven teeth pulled due to severe periodontal disease. When she was no longer able to have as many puppies as was deemed profitable, she was dropped off at a high-kill shelter, where she would have been killed if she hadn't been saved by RR. It was through RR that Cheryl first heard about Taffy and adopted her. "Something about her face tugged at my heartstrings. When I learned her story, I knew she needed to come live with my mom and me." Having lived her entire life in an outdoor cage, Taffy now needed to adjust to life in a home. She was fearful of strangers at first but has since learned that people are fun. She also had to learn to play. Now a warm and loving member of the family, Taffy has come a long way. When people meet her, they don't believe she ever lived in a puppy mill—the only proof is the tattoos in her ears, which were the breeder's identification marks. She now loves squeaky toys, kisses and belly rubs. Taffy also likes to steal people's socks and hoard them. Cheryl's mother is legally blind, and Taffy has taken on the role of being her personal guard and caretaker. When Cheryl leaves the house, she tells Taffy to "take care of GrandMargie," and little Taffy jumps in her mom's lap.

A puppy mill is an inhumane commercial dog-breeding facility in which profits are maximized by cutting overhead costs. The health and welfare of the animals is not a consideration.

To maximize profits, mill owners keep the breeder dogs in cramped wire-floor crates. To minimize the cost of care needed for these dogs, the dogs are not played with or walked. Because the crates are stacked on top of each other, the dogs in the lower crates are forced to endure urine and feces "raining down" on them from the crates above. Most of the dogs are forced to live in their own waste. Many mill dogs are kept outside with no protection from the elements.

The mill owners further minimize overhead and maximize profits by giving the dogs poor-quality dog food and little to no medical care. The dogs are often infested with parasites.

Most of these dogs never receive affection and never know life outside their crates. Breeder dogs pulled from mills typically have to learn how to play.

Puppy mills will breed female dogs every time they are in heat. This overbreeding causes medical issues. Once the dogs are no longer able to produce enough puppies to be considered profitable, the dogs are disposed of, inhumanely put down, abandoned, dropped off at shelters or sold at auction to other mill owners.

Mill puppies, because the mill owners have no concern for the quality of dog they are producing, are often inbred and as a result may have genetic deformities and/or conditions, and psychological or physiological issues. They typically are malnourished, infested with parasites, and/or are ill.

Under the federal Animal Welfare Act, it is completely legal to keep a dog in a cage only 6 inches longer than the dog in each direction, with a wire floor, stacked on top of another cage, for the dog's entire life. Although these are conditions that most people would consider inhumane, they are often completely legal. Only 26 states have laws that regulate commercial kennels to prevent animal abuse and cruelty. However, in most cases, the standards that breeders are required to meet by law are minimal.

Almost all puppies sold in pet stores or sold online are bought from puppy mills. A consumer who purchases a puppy from a pet store is usually given falsified information about the dog's health, lineage, breed and breeder. By purchasing a pet-store puppy, you are not saving a puppy-mill dog. Instead, you are supporting the very business model that keeps the puppy mills in operation. You are putting money in the pockets of the puppy-mill owners and thus condemning your puppy's parents, and the thousands of dogs just like them, to lives of misery and suffering.

Because most puppy mills are not illegal, the way to put an end to puppy mills is to stop the demand for their product. You can help by agreeing to never buy a dog from a pet store or online. Consider adopting your next pet from a shelter. There are many breed-specific rescues that can help you find your next dog. If you decide to buy a dog from a breeder, make sure you have carefully screened the breeder in person. Screening includes meeting the puppy's parents, seeing how the animals are kept and getting references from previous clients.

The ASPCA estimates that there could be as many as 10,000 puppy mills in the United States.

Sources: The Humane Society of the United States and ASPCA websites.

ADVOCACY GROUPS, ANIMAL RESCUES & EDUCATIONAL WEBSITES

Animal Rescue Corps | animalrescuecorps.org/learn/puppy-mills
ASPCA | nopetstorepuppies.com
Best Friends Animal Society | bestfriends.org/Resources/No-Kill-Resources/Puppy-Mills
Cuda Cares | facebook.com/cudacaresorg
Hearts United for Animals | hua.org
Humane Society of the United States | humanesociety.org/issues/puppy_mills
Main Line Animal Rescue | mlar.org
National Mill Dog Rescue | milldogrescue.org
New Rattitude Rat Terrier Rescue | newrattitude.org
No More Tears Rescue | nomoretearsrescue.com
North Shore Animal League America | animalleague.org/rescue/pet-rescue-programs/puppy-mill-rescue
Puppy Mill Project | thepuppymillproject.org
United Against Puppy Mills | unitedagainstpuppymills.org

BOOKS

Dog Blessed: Puppy Mill Survivor Stories by Lisa Fischer
Puppy Mill Dogs SPEAK!: Happy Stories and Helpful Advice by Christine Palm Shaughness
Saving Gracie: How One Dog Escaped the Shadowy World of American Puppy Mills by Carol Bradley

FILMS & DOCUMENTARIES

I'm Alive For The Very First Time
Madonna of the Mills | madonnaofthemills.com
Prisoners of Greed | prisonersofgreed.org

Resources

THE PROJECTS WISH TO THANK THE FOLLOWING
BUSINESSES & ORGANIZATIONS FOR THEIR SUPPORT.

ANIMAL RESCUE
New Rattitude Rat Terrier Rescue | newrattitude.org (national rescue)
Paws 4 You Rescue — Miami, FL | paws4you.org (nonprofit dog rescue)
SPCA of Northern Virginia | spcanova.org (foster-based animal rescue)

CHILDREN'S BOOKS
Louie, The Little Blue Dog by Karen Roberts | thelittlebluedog.com

DOG TRAINING
AngelDogs Training — Santa Clarita, CA | angeldogstraining.com
      (CPDT Dog Training, Canine Good Citizen Evaluator)
Happy Urban Dog — Land O' Lakes, FL | happyurbandog.com
In Tune Dogs — Northeast GA | intunedogs.com

PET SITTING
Amanda's Pet Care — Arlington, VA | amandaspetcare.com

PROSTHETIC CARE
Prosthetic Care Facility of Virginia joins the fight to put an end to puppy mills | prostheticcarefacility.com

VETERINARY HOSPITAL
Pecan Acres Pet Care — Lake Jackson, TX | pecanacrespetcare.com

THE PROJECTS WISH TO THANK THE FOLLOWING
PEOPLE FOR THEIR SUPPORT

Amanda, Steven & Zuma Carlson — Arlington, VA
Andrew & Cindy Tokar, For our first rescue, "Alex," a puppy-mill rescue — Redmond, WA
Anne Ferara, For my GSDs Myah & Magnum — Cherry Hill, NJ
Carm & the Girls — Campbellville, ON, Canada
Cindy & Robbie Szakos, In loving memory of Hunter, Snickers, Coco & Noki — PA
Dawn Blair, In loving memory of my little man, Little Niki — Richmond, VA
Emily thanks Deborah, Neale & All Pets for her forever home — LA
Erin-Kaye Dodge, For my Kidz (past, present & future) — Greeley, CO
George, Karen, Sarah & Biscuit Nagel. We miss our beloved Lola — Marietta, GA
Heather Jirgensen, In memory of Luke, Schatzee & Carmen — Racine, WI
Jamie, Courtney & Lawson Canine, For our wonderful pup, Bentley! — Columbia, MO
Jessica Peretti, Lily & Eli — Chicago, IL
Joe Kotch, In honor of Nina, Sula & Prince — PA
Joe Kotch, In memory of Sage, Bella & Shadow — PA
Judy Foszcz, For Apollo — Ingleside, IL
Julee & Brett Allen, For our rescued Rat Terrier Catty — Seattle, WA
Julie Campbell — Seattle, WA
Karen Pederson & all my "rescues" — CA
Karen Seydel — CA
Kristi Gross, Gypsy & Panda — Dallas, TX
Kym Sargent, In memory of ~My Beau~ — Trinity, AL
Leslie Phillips, For my Kizzy Butt — Las Vegas, NV
Libby Welles, For sweet little Sofi — Las Vegas, NV
The Lindorfer Pack — Salem, OR
Michelle Weirich, For Denise DeMarco, my friend who has saved 100s of dogs from dying in horrible
     puppy mills! — PA
Rick & Mary Beth Brown, In memory of Petey — St. Louis, MO
The Rinicker Family, For Lilly — Land O' Lakes, FL
The Tatur Family, For our beloved Silver & Sebastian — South Tamworth, NH
Tina Austin & The Hairbabies: Bandit, Missy, Reily & Callie — Tacoma, WA

Rescues & Shelters

THE FOLLOWING ENTITIES ARE RESPONSIBLE FOR SAVING THE DOGS IN THIS BOOK

all rover's rescue friends | allroversrescuefriends.org

cavalier rescue usa | cavalierrescueusa.org

greater birmingham humane society | gbhs.org

home for friendless animals | friendlessanimals.com

humane society of the united states | humanesociety.org

internet miniature pinscher service | minpinrescue.org

meriden humane society | members.petfinder.com/~CT20/Home.htm

midwest dachshund rescue | mwdr.org

national mill dog rescue | milldogrescue.org

new rattitude rat terrier rescue | newrattitude.org

north shore animal league america | animalleague.org

petfinder | petfinder.com

ratbone rescues | ratbonerescues.com

richmond indiana animal control

rolling dog farm | rollingdogfarm.org

washington animal rescue league | warl.org

whippet rescue and placement (louisiana) | whippet-rescue.com

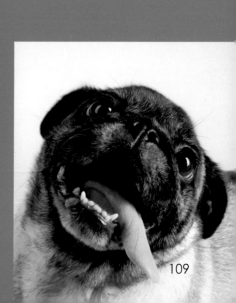

What started as an idea for one photo book on deaf dogs back in August 2008 developed into a series of photo books, with this book, *Puppy-Mill Survivors*, being the fourth in the series. The core message in each book is that we need to open our hearts and minds to those animals we might have preconceptions about and those who need our help, whether that is deaf dogs, shelter/rescue dogs, pit bulls or puppy-mill dogs. The product line of calendars, cards and prints all spread the vital message that these dogs are individuals...treat them as such. The puppy-mill photo book took me on another countrywide road trip with my deaf dog, Sadie. This trip lasted 5 weeks. That trip was then followed by much smaller and shorter trips on the East Coast.

BOOKS IN THE SERIES:

Deaf Dogs
Rescued in America
Pit Bulls & Pit Bull Type Dogs
Puppy-Mill Survivors

STATS FOR PUPPY-MILL SURVIVORS:

Duration of photo sessions: 8 months
(Oct. 2009; Jan. 2010; Aug. 2010; May 2011 - Jul. 2011; Sept. 2012; Feb. 2013)
Number of road trips taken during that time: 8
Number of states dogs were photographed in: 13
Number of dogs photographed for *Puppy-Mill Survivors*: 33

TOTAL STATS FOR ALL 4 BOOKS:

Duration of photo sessions: 25 months
(Feb. 2009 - Apr. 2010; Aug. 2010; Mar. 2011 - Sept. 2011; Sept. 2012; Feb. 2013)
Number of road trips taken during that time: 43
Approximate miles traveled: 45,785
Number of states traversed during the trips: 45
Number of provinces traversed during the trips: 2
Number of states dogs were photographed in: 37
Number of provinces dogs were photographed in: 1
Total number of dogs in all 4 books: 298
Number of dogs photographed for *Deaf Dogs*: 78
Number of dogs photographed for *Rescued in America*: 105
Number of dogs photographed for *Pit Bulls & Pit Bull Type Dogs*: 82

www.thephotobooks.com

The Photo Book Projects

Special Thanks to...

egil nilsson
sadie
gary crews & everyone at cpc solutions
jim dew & everyone at roswell bookbinding
kristin walinski

the following people, businesses & organizations for hosting photo shoots:
    ahimsa dog training
    the big bad woof
    debbie & marc maas
    dogone fun
    grisha stewart
    new rattitude rat terrier rescue
    north shore animal league america

new rattitude rat terrier rescue & north shore animal league america for their pre-publication support of this book

the hundreds of people who pre-ordered the books and spread the word about the project

the people lucky enough to be owned by the dogs in this book

the individuals, businesses, shelters & rescues that supported & promoted the project

the sponsors for their support & belief in the project

a special thanks to julee allen, kat kostro, kristi gross & new rattitude rat terrier rescue for their generous support of the project